MW00761036

Step Right Up

What Your Shoes Can Teach You

Step Right Up

What Your Shoes Can Teach You

TARGUM/FELDHEIM

First published 2001
Copyright © 2001 by Moshe Goldberger
ISBN 1-56871-262-6

Published by:
Targum Press, Inc.
22700 W. Eleven Mile Rd.
Southfield, MI 48034
E-mail: targum@netvision.net.il
Fax: 888-298-9992
www.targum.com

Distributed by:
Feldheim Publishers
202 Airport Executive Park
Nanuet, NY 10954

Printed in Israel

With thanks to:
Rabbi Eliezer Gevirtz
Rabbi Menachem Goldman
Mordechai Gelber
Yitzchok E. Gold
B. Siegel
Dr. J. Cohen
and others

Contents

LESSONS FROM OUR SHOES

Introduction 11
1. Thanking for Shoes 13
2. Walking with the Wise 15
3. Five Forms of Pleasure 18
4. Excommunication 20
5. The Shoe Strap of Avraham 22
6. Remove Your Shoes 24
7. A Step in the Right Direction 26
8. A Heel 28
9. Footnotes 30
10. *Chalitzah* 33
11. The First Shoe Manufacturer 35
12. *Chesed* with One's Shoes 37
13. Be Prepared with Shoes on Your Feet . . 40
14. Body and Soul 42
15. Beautiful Shoes 44
16. The Source of All 47
17. Shoes and *Shidduchim* 49
18. Footsteps in History 52

19. The Shoe Connection. 55
20. Making Shoes versus Writing Books . . 58
21. Putting on Shoes 60
22. Step by Step 62
23. Touching Shoes 64
24. A Closer Look at Handling Shoes 66
25. Shoes on Shabbos 68
26. Cleaning Shoes on Shabbos 72
27. Shoes on Yom Kippur 74
28. Shoes on Chol HaMo'ed 76
29. Miscellaneous Shoe Halachos 78

TEN BLESSINGS

1. Gift of a Mind 83
2. Gift of Identity 85
3. Gift of Freedom 87
4. Gift of More Mitzvah Opportunities . . . 89
5. Gift of Eyesight 91
6. Gift of Clothing 93
7. Gift of Mobility 95
8. Gift of Upright Posture 97
9. Gift of the Ground 99
10. Gift of Shoes 101
    Epilogue 103

Part One

Lessons from Our Shoes

Introduction

Every morning, we recite a list of blessings, thanking Hashem for so many aspects of our lives. The blessing that seems to be the most significant of them all loudly proclaims our thanks to Hashem "for providing us with all our needs." What an amazing and powerful statement!

But our Sages inform us that this blessing refers specifically to our shoes (*Berachos* 60b). This is quite surprising. Why zero in on shoes when the blessing seems to be all-encompassing?

This question has led us on a search through Tanach and Chazal to study the subject of shoes and uncover their importance. The profound lessons that we have gleaned are contained in the following pages.

Chapter One

Thanking for Shoes

The Gemara states, "When a person puts on his shoes, he says, 'Blessed are You, Hashem... who has provided me with all my needs'" (*Berachos* 60b).

This halachah is quoted in the *Shulchan Aruch* (*Orach Chaim* 46:1), which then adds that nowadays we say all the morning *berachos* at one time before *shacharis*. The *Mishnah Berurah* explains that the concept behind this blessing is that one may not enjoy a pleasure in this world without first thanking Hashem.

All too often, we take for granted the gifts Hashem has given us. Rabbi Avigdor Miller, *zt"l*, reminds us that we need to be appreciative of the fact that our shoes today are of durable and comfortable material, dyed pleasing colors, polished, and lined inside for comfort. Our shoes are designed and fashioned by skilled artisans and made from materials gathered from great distances. They have hard soles to protect the feet and rubber heels for comfortable walking, and their laces are tipped with metal or plastic for convenient use (*Rejoice O Youth*, p. 313).

All of these thoughts and more are well worth considering when we voice our daily thank you to Hashem for our shoes.

The Talmud teaches that one should even sell the beams of his house, if necessary, in order to purchase shoes for his feet (*Shabbos* 129a). A second version of this teaching, which Rashi quotes in *Pesachim* (112a), is even more emphatic: A person should even sell everything he owns in order to buy a pair of shoes.

Why are shoes so important? Avudraham explains that shoes enable a person to go out to take care of all his other needs. Our Sages are thus teaching us to appreciate everything we have been given as a result of our shoes.

Chapter Two

Walking with the Wise

Shoes enable us to walk more easily and to perform numerous mitzvos that involve our feet. The Talmud (*Kesubos* 111a) teaches that a person should spend a third of his time walking, a third sitting, and a third standing to promote his overall health and welfare.

Some of the mitzvos we use our feet for include:

- Standing up for parents, teachers, and elderly people
- Standing up for a *sefer Torah*
- Standing during *Shemoneh Esrei*
- Escorting guests
- Dancing in honor of a groom and bride
- Visiting the sick and mourners

Performing these mitzvos will put us in the category of those who "walk before Hashem"

(*Tehillim* 116:9). In addition, we learn, "He who walks with the wise will become wise" (*Mishlei* 13:20).

The Gemara (*Sukkah* 49b) quotes a verse in *Shir HaShirim* (7:2): "How beautiful are your footsteps in shoes, daughter of the noble one." This refers to the footsteps of the Jews when they walked three times a year to celebrate the festivals in Yerushalayim. People would wear special shoes for *aliyah l'regel*, the long mitzvah trek they would embark on three times a year (*Targum Onkelos* loc. cit.).

Although *regel* refers to the three holidays on which we are commanded to ascend to the Beis HaMikdash, it also literally means "foot." According to the Malbim (on *Shemos* 23:14–17), *aliyah l'regel* would train the Jews to walk for and with Hashem.

The Torah describes Noach as "walking with Hashem" (*Bereishis* 6:9). What does this mean? Noach always trained himself to be aware of Hashem and to behave as one who is in the presence of the king.

Similarly, Hashem instructs Avraham Avinu, "Walk before Me and become perfect" (ibid. 17:1). This teaches us that being aware of Hashem's presence is the greatest way to reach perfection. Thinking of Hashem, the All-Powerful Creator of the Universe, fortifies us against the temptations that distract us from our duties in this world. In addition, focusing on fear and love of Hashem helps us become more righteous and more praise-worthy (Rabbeinu Yonah, *Shaarei Teshuvah* 2:1).

Chapter Three

Five Forms of Pleasure

On Yom Kippur, the holiest day of the year, we are commanded to refrain from five forms of pleasure.

The Mishnah teaches: "On Yom Kippur it is forbidden to eat and drink, bathe or wash, apply lotion, wear leather shoes, and have marital relations" (*Yoma* 73b).

These afflictions assist us in our repentance and help incline our hearts to submit themselves to Hashem. We also learn to appreciate these forms of pleasure which are permitted on the other days of the year. Although it is easy to take these pleasures for granted, they are actually primary pleasures which can be enjoyed daily.

Since we are focusing on shoes in this book, we urge you to begin a program of appreciating your shoes and the blessing linked to them. When you take a walk today, pause for a few moments to say to yourself, *Wow! What a benefit these shoes are. Thank You, Hashem, for this gift.*

Chapter Four

Excommunication

The Gemara (*Pesachim* 113b) teaches that seven types of people are excommunicated by Heaven. They are:

1. One who refuses to marry

2. One who refuses to have children (see *Tosafos*)

3. One who refuses to teach his children Torah

4. One who refuses to wear tefillin

5. One who refuses to put tzitzis on his four-cornered garments

6. One who refuses to put mezuzos on the doors of his rooms

7. One who refuses to wear shoes

The inclusion of one who refuses to wear shoes in the above list is a clear indication of the critical role shoes play in our lives, not only in this world but also the next.

As we will see, shoes serve many functions. Not only do they serve us physically, but they also provide many fundamental spiritual lessons. In this *gemara*, on a basic level, shoes signify caring for one's physical needs. One who refuses to do so is held accountable.

As Jews, we know that every aspect of our lives should be part of our service to Hashem. Caring for one's body by wearing shoes is a precious mitzvah which is important enough to include in this list of some of the greatest mitzvos.

Chapter Five

The Shoe Strap of Avraham

Where are shoes first mentioned in the Torah?

When Avraham Avinu turned down war spoils after his miraculous conquest of four enemy nations, he declared, "Not even a thread or a shoe strap, I will not take anything of yours" (*Bereishis* 14:23). Rashi (on *Sotah* 17a) explains that although the property was legally his, as the Talmud teaches (*Bava Kama* 114a), Avraham refused to accept it because he wished to distance himself from goods that had originally been stolen.

The Gemara declares: "In reward for Avraham's statement, 'Not even a thread or a shoe strap,' Avraham's descendants merited two mitzvos: the thread of *techeiles* in the tzitzis and the straps of tefillin" (*Sotah* 17a).

What is the connection between Avraham's refusal and these two mitzvos we have merited?

Avraham's reason for not accepting the war booty was "so that you do not say, 'I made Avraham wealthy'" (*Bereishis* 14:23). Avraham understood that the ultimate source of all wealth is Hashem, and only Hashem. The garments we wear and the leather of our shoes are also gifts to us from Hashem to demonstrate that we are superior to plants and animals. All plant and animal life was created in order to serve our needs.

The leather of a shoe strap is similar to the leather of tefillin (just as the thread Avraham referred to is similar to the *techeiles* of tzitzis) in that they both elevate us by demonstrating that we are chosen by Hashem to serve Him, and that all the rest of creation is intended to serve us.

When Hashem spoke to Moshe Rabbeinu
for the first time at the burning bush,
He said, "Do not approach here. Remove your shoes from your feet, for the ground
you are standing on is holy" (*Shemos* 3:5).

We find a similar instruction in *Sefer
Yehoshua* (5:15), when an angel encounters
Yehoshua and instructs him to remove his shoes.
The Midrash teaches us the principle that when-
ever there is a revelation of the Divine Presence,
one may not wear shoes (*Shemos Rabbah* 2:13).

This brings us to an intriguing question. Why
did our Sages establish a daily blessing to be re-
cited for shoes if it is inappropriate to wear shoes
in Hashem's Presence?

When David HaMelech wanted to demonstrate his subservience to Hashem, he walked
barefoot (*Shmuel* II 15:30), and the *kohanim* were

orbidden to wear shoes when they served in the
Beis HaMikdash.

These examples reflect that although wearing
shoes represents our dominion over all other crea-
tures, when it comes to serving Hashem we remove our shoes to demonstrate Hashem's dominion over us. We humble ourselves before the Creator, who grants us all the power we have.

Another lesson to be learned from the command to remove one's shoes in a holy place is that
one should surrender his ego to the sanctity of
such a place. Rav Shamshon Refael Hirsch
teaches that Moshe and Yehoshua were instructed to devote themselves to their lofty desti-
nies, symbolized by the ground upon which they
stood. As we learn from *Mishlei* (17:24), "Wisdom
is in front of an understanding person, whereas a
fool's eyes search to the end of the earth." Don't let
your ego prevent you from seeing the opportunities for holiness that surround you.

Chapter Seven

A Step in the Right Direction

I n describing the conquest of Eretz Yisrael to the Jewish people, Moshe tells them, "Every place where the sole of your foot shall tread shall be yours..." (*Devarim* 11:24).

Why does the Torah use the graphic illustration of footsteps in describing this conquest?

One has to demonstrate his positive intentions with his footsteps.

> *He who comes to purify himself will be assisted by Hashem.*
>
> (*Shabbos* 104a)

> *On the path one desires to go, he will be led.*
>
> (*Makkos* 10b)

The key words in these quotes are *comes* and *to go*. If one desires a path but stays in his place and doesn't take steps in that direction, he is demonstrating his lack of sincerity.

The words *rotzeh* (desires) and *ratz* (runs) share a common root. This is because we show our desire by running in its direction.

When the Jewish nation took steps in the Land, thus demonstrating their intention to fulfill Hashem's word, He assisted them in conquering the land. We learn from this the necessity and value of even mere steps in the right direction. Hashem desires to see some attempt to succeed on our part (Rav Avigdor Miller, *Fortunate Nation*, p. 184). Then He responds by blessing us "in all that we do" (*Devarim* 15:18).

Chapter Eight

A Heel

Would you name your son after a heel? The Torah tells us the origin of our forefather Yaakov's name is from the word *heel*: "His hand was holding Eisav's heel" (*Bereishis* 25:26).

The truth is the name is not as bad as it sounds. We learn that it was a prophetic message that Yaakov will overcome Eisav. In the time of David HaMelech, all of Edom, Eisav's descendants, became servants to David (*Shmuel* II 8:14), and the same will occur in the future, as we are taught, "The saviors shall ascend Mount Zion to judge Mount Eisav" (*Ovadyah* 1:21).

Yaakov receives eternal rewards, as the Talmud teaches, "All Jews have a share in the World to Come" (*Sanhedrin* 90a).

The heel is a metaphor for the results, the conclusion (see *Devarim* 7:12). Yaakov, the last of the forefathers, symbolizes the final glories of the future for the nation that is most loyal to Hashem and His Torah.

Chapter Nine

Footnotes

There are many inspiring stories that illustrate the power of even the most minute details of Torah law. We should not take lightly even those halachos that seem trivial in our limited vision, as the following story about shoes illustrates.

There was a yeshivah day school rebbe who taught his class the laws of dressing in the morning, including the practice of putting on first the right shoe, then the left, and then tying the left shoe first. Some of the parent body was opposed to their children learning such seemingly trivial points rather than more basic tenets of Judaism, and one boy was actually pulled out of the school shortly afterwards.

As this boy grew older, he tragically strayed from Judaism. He eventually became engaged to a non-Jewish woman.

As he was dressing one morning a few weeks before his impending wedding, he realized that he had a specific way of putting on his shoes. First he put on his right shoe, then the left, and then he tied the left before the right. It was an ingrained habit that caused him to remember his day school lessons and that he was a Jew with responsibilities to his Creator. Even though he had strayed, what he had learned had stayed with him and was still a part of him.

He realized he could not go through with the wedding with a clear conscience. Much to everyone's surprise, he broke off the engagement and began to look into and rediscover his background (Rabbi Yosef Weiss, *Visions of Greatness*, vol. 2 [Lakewood: CIS, 1996], p. 193).

Another shoe story is recorded in *Nifleosav Livnei Adam* by Baruch Lev (p. 121).

A nonreligious Jewish soldier met a *frum* Jew in the course of his travels. The observant person shared some aspects of *Yiddishkeit* with his fellow Jew, who became inspired by the information and took it upon himself to accept one halachah from the *Shulchan Aruch*, since this would serve as a great merit for survival in battle.

He took upon himself to begin putting his

shoes on correctly, as described in the *Shulchan Aruch*. The halachah seemed fairly simple to him, and he fulfilled it every day. When he did forget once in a while, he would return to his barracks to remove his shoes and put them on again properly.

One day he left his company's line-up to put his shoes on correctly, since he had forgotten to do so that morning. This time he was caught leaving the line-up and penalized with detention.

That day his regiment went out on a mission, and he was left behind. The enemy ambushed them and all the soldiers were killed. This soldier's commitment to the shoe mitzvah had saved his life.

Chapter Ten

Chalitzah

I f a man dies, leaving his widow childless, his brother is commanded to marry the widow and thus perform the mitzvah of *yibum*. If he refuses to do so, she has to remove his shoe, spit on the ground in front of him, and say, "This is what is done to the man who refuses to build up his brother's home." And then all the observers announce, "The shoe has been removed" (*Devarim* 25:5–10). (Nowadays, *yibum* is not an option and *chalitzah* is always the required procedure.)

What is the significance of this unique ceremony?

The Malbim quotes a Talmudic teaching in explanation: "Riding a horse was the symbol of a king, riding a donkey was a sign of an independent person, and wearing shoes shows one is a human being" (*Shabbos* 152a).

The main difference between humans and animals is that people have the free will to choose how to behave. We wear shoes of leather to demonstrate that we are superior to the animals, who walk on the bare earth. The leather, made of animal hide, demonstrates our power to utilize animal parts for our needs. Shoes are symbolic of the dignity of man.

A person's ability to differentiate right from wrong gives him the ability to decide to serve Hashem, and thus overcome his animalistic tendencies which attempt to persuade him otherwise. Thus, in this case where a person is refusing to follow the Torah's ideal, the mitzvah of *yibum*, his sister-in-law removes his shoe to demonstrate that he is not utilizing his superiority and thus does not deserve to wear his shoe.

Chapter Eleven

The First Shoe Manufacturer

Chanoch was a righteous shoemaker who would focus on serving Hashem with every stitch he sewed.

(*Midrash Talpiyos*)

Rav Yisrael Salanter explains this to mean that as Chanoch would manufacture each shoe he was careful to perform each step properly in order to provide people with good, strong shoes. He was careful not to cheat any of his customers in any way. Thus, he focused on serving Hashem in the highest fashion in every step of the way (*Da'as Chochmah U'Mussar* 1:204).

This lesson applies to all of us in whatever business or profession we are involved with. We need to always focus on meeting Hashem's standards and fulfilling the halachos that apply to us in every endeavor. May we merit "to walk with Hashem's laws" (*Vayikra* 26:3) and to experience fulfillment of the truism: "On the path one desires to go, he will be led" (*Makkos* 10b).

Chapter Twelve

Chesed with One's Shoes

The following story was told by Rav Nassan Wachtfogel, *zt"l*, regarding Rav Simchah Zissel Ziv, the great sage of Kelm, who was famous for his great wisdom and his emphasis on *mussar*. Always striving for self-perfection, Reb Simchah Zissel knew Rabbeinu Yonah's *Shaarei Teshuvah* by heart.

One night, Reb Simchah Zissel had a dream that Rabbeinu Yonah had come to his town to deliver a discourse in the local shul. Reb Simchah Zissel rushed to the shul to hear the lecture, but to his dismay they would not let him in.

He tried to come up with a merit that would allow him inside, but no matter what he said he could not gain entry. Finally, he mentioned that he had a son named Nachum Zev. Immediately, he was admitted to the shul. At that point he awoke from his dream.

Reb Simchah Zissel went to his son to relate the dream and ask him what unique mitzvah he had done recently that would serve as a source of merit for his father.

Nachum Zev related that his old boots were falling apart. He had been desperate to purchase a new pair and saved up money for it for weeks. The night after he bought his new pair of boots, a poor man knocked on the door asking for some charity. Nachum Zev noticed that the man was standing in the snow barefoot. "I gave him my new boots and went back to wearing my old ones," he explained (Rabbi Yosef Weiss, *Visions of Greatness*, vol. 1 [Lakewood: CIS, 1993], p. 75).

Another story involving shoes is found in Rav Paysach Krohn's book, *In the Footsteps of the Maggid* (New York: ArtScroll/Mesorah, 1992, p. 144).

Rebbetzin Chana Munk would collect charity for the needy from all of the houses of her town. She was concerned that some people would not be able to give but would feel embarrassed to say so when she came by. Her solution was to buy a pair of heavy wooden clogs to wear when making her collection rounds. When she approached a home, people knew it was her and they could ignore her knock if they were unable to help out.

These are two examples of how you can use your shoes not only to carry out daily activities, but also to help others.

Chapter Thirteen

Be Prepared
with Shoes on Your Feet

*This is how you shall eat it [the korban
pesach]: with your belts tight, shoes on your
feet, your walking stick in your hand, and you
will eat quickly; it is Pesach for Hashem.*

(*Shemos* 12:11)

This was the command given to the Jewish
people in Egypt before their exodus. Rashi
explains the Jews were to eat already prepared for travel. Rav Avigdor Miller (*A Nation Is
Born*, p. 125) explains three lessons that we learn
from this mitzvah, which was performed in a hasty
manner:

1. We need to always be alert in life to run away
   from evil influences, as we are taught in *Avos*
   4:2 — "Run to perform even easy mitzvos, and
   flee from sin."

2. The nation was eager to go to Sinai, where it would receive Hashem's Torah. This would be the fulfillment of the great proclamation: "Send out My people so that they serve Me" (*Shemos* 7:16).

3. This is a demonstration of Hashem's mighty hand when He intervened on behalf of the freedom of His people. "I am Hashem; in its time I shall hasten it [the redemption]" (*Yeshayah* 60:2).

Chapter Fourteen

Body and Soul

When Naomi sent Rus to Boaz's threshing grounds for the purpose of asking him to perform the mitzvah of *yibum*, she instructed her, "When he goes to lie down...go and uncover his feet" (*Rus* 3:4).

The Malbim explains this with an insight from Kabbalah: The body of a person in this world is considered the "shoe" of the *neshamah*. That is why Moshe Rabbeinu was instructed to remove his shoes at the burning bush. This was a symbolic message to leave his body behind and spiritually elevate himself in order to communicate with Hashem.

In this vein, when a person dies without children, it is as if he needs someone to step into his shoes to help him perpetuate his name in this world. If *chalitzah* is performed instead of *yibum*, it symbolizes that the brother does not wish to be a "shoe provider" for his deceased brother. This was the hint Rus was giving to Boaz: "Please accept this mitzvah to marry me and save my husband. Cover your feet with us, so to speak."

This provides us with another, deeper approach to understanding all the above-mentioned sources regarding shoes. Shoes are symbolic of touching the ground, being in contact with the physical world. Although the physical world on the surface level is antithetical to our service of Hashem, we need to provide for our physical needs if we want to live and serve Hashem properly. We are taught in *Avos* (3:17): "If there is no flour [i.e., food], there will not be Torah."

We should not ignore our physical needs. Fulfilling them is necessary for making strides in the spiritual world.

Chapter Fifteen

Beautiful Shoes

*How beautiful are your footsteps in shoes,
daughter of the noble one.*

(*Shir HaShirim* 7:2)

Why are shoes mentioned in this verse? The Gemara (*Chagigah* 3a) explains this verse as a reference to the Jews traveling to the Beis HaMikdash three times a year for the holidays of Pesach, Shavuos, and Sukkos. We are described as descendants of Avraham Avinu, who was the founder of our nation or, as the Gemara says, the first convert to Judaism.

The Midrash says that one of the rewards that Avraham merited when he refused to keep any of the war spoils after defeating the four kings was the mitzvah of *aliyah l'regel*. Because he refused even a shoe strap, his children merited the shoes they used for traveling long distances to fulfill this mitzvah.

The unique relationship that we as a nation have with Hashem began when Hashem tested Avraham with the supreme test of the *akeidah*, the command to sacrifice his son Yitzchak (*Bereishis* 22:1).

At the climax of the *akeidah*, Avraham called the mountain where he was prepared to sacrifice Yitzchak "Hashem sees" (ibid., 14). The verse continues, "As it is said until today, 'At the mountain where Hashem is seen.' " This alludes to the precept, "Three times a year shall all of your males be seen before Hashem, the Master" (*Shemos* 23:17, 34:23).

The Beis HaMikdash eventually built on this same mountain taught people that Hashem sees all, provides for all, and rewards and punishes all. We come "to be seen" by Hashem three times a year to remind ourselves that Hashem always sees us. The reward for our remembering Hashem is Hashem's bestowal of His blessings on us.

But why is it necessary to serve Hashem on a mountain? Is there any difference if we bring an offering to Hashem on a mountain or in a valley? Hashem wants us to serve Him in the way that will make the greatest impression upon us. When we ascend a mountain, we feel as if we are coming closer to Hashem. This increased awareness of Hashem causes us to come closer to Him in the spiritual sense (Rav Avigdor Miller, *The Beginning*, p. 350).

This may be one explanation why the verse in *Shir HaShirim* referring to *aliyah l'regel* mentions shoes. A person prepares himself for a long trip by getting a good pair of walking shoes. Hashem, who sees all, appreciates our efforts to perform mitzvos and praises us for them.

In addition, the Targum on *Shir HaShirim* says that the Jews would wear colorful shoes for this mitzvah. This is explained as a fulfillment of the precept to perform every mitzvah with *hiddur* (beauty), another means of coming closer to Hashem.

Chapter Sixteen

The Source of All

The Torah teaches us that Avraham said to the king of Sedom, "I lift up my hand [in a vow] to Hashem, the Supreme God, Creator of heaven and earth, that I will not take even a thread or a shoe strap..." (*Bereishis* 14:22–23).

Tanna D'vei Eliyahu, Zuta, ch. 25, teaches that when Avraham Avinu made this proclamation, Hashem kissed his hands and said, "From the Day of Creation until today, you are the first one who recognized Me as 'Hashem, the Supreme God.' "

Avraham had demonstrated his understanding of Hashem's complete mastery over everything in this world, including every single bit of wealth a person earns.

From the Midrash (*Bereishis Rabbah* 43:13) we learn that there is a measure-for-measure connection between Avraham's refusal to accept shoe straps from Sedom and the mitzvah of *aliyah l'regel*. Avraham's refusal was based on his extreme closeness to Hashem. He was determined to avoid any possible *chillul Hashem* and didn't want the Sedomites to say, "We made Avraham wealthy" (*Bereishis* 14:23). When we forsake our fields and homes three times a year to acknowledge that Hashem is the sole Owner of the land, He promises, in return, to make sure that no one will take our land while we are away (*Shemos* 34:24).

Chapter Seventeen

Shoes and Shidduchim

*A person should sell all that he owns [if neces-
sary] in order to marry the daughter of a Torah
scholar...so that his children will grow up to be
Torah scholars.... He should also sell everything he owns...to marry off his daughter to a
Torah scholar....*

(Pesachim 49a)

We have studied earlier a similar statement from our Sages regarding buying
shoes. What is the connection between
selling everything to buy shoes and selling everything in order to marry the right type of woman?

We have discussed the concept behind the
daily blessing for shoes, "Blessed are You...who
has provided me with all my needs." What an appropriate comparison to a wife, regarding whom
the Torah teaches, "A man should therefore forsake his father and mother and cling to his wife,

and they will become one flesh" (*Bereishis* 2:24). A husband and wife are each other's completion. She is the foundation of his person, a part of him, and they help each other to perfect their characters. The word *cling* (*davak*) is also used in reference to Hashem (*Devarim* 10:20), because a wife helps perfect her husband's personality so that together they merit to become attached to Hashem.

The *Gemara* teaches that if a man told a woman that he would marry her with the understanding that he has a certain level of *yichus* (lineage) but then it is discovered that he is actually more distinguished, the marriage is not valid (*Kiddushin* 49a). Why? Because the woman can say, "I'm not interested in a shoe that is too large for my foot. I cannot walk with it."

We again see a reference to shoes in this metaphor, which shows how a *shidduch* is compared to a properly fitting shoe. Hashem provides us with all our needs, and Shlomo HaMelech teaches us, "He who finds a wife finds good, and he obtains favor from Hashem" (*Mishlei* 18:22).

The Gemara (*Yevamos* 63a) teaches us two vital lessons in finding a mate:

- Be patient to find the right woman. (*Rashi* —

Wait until you examine her ways and see if she is negative or contrary.)

• Go down a step to marry the right one. (*Rashi* — Do not marry a woman who is of a higher status than you, for you may not be acceptable to her.)

If the shoe is too big it may fall off. For long term success, it is important that the shoe should fit just right.

Chapter Eighteen

Footsteps in History

The rewards for the mitzvah of escorting others on their way, even if one only goes a short distance, are unlimited. The Gemara (*Sotah* 46b) illustrates this principle with three amazing historical episodes:

"Pharaoh instructed his people to escort Avraham, his wife, and all of his possessions" (*Bereishis* 12:20). Pharaoh was demonstrating his penitence in order to mitigate Hashem's wrath against him for his kidnaping of Sarah. He therefore sent Avraham and Sarah away with honor.

As a reward for taking four steps with Avraham, Pharaoh was given the power to subjugate the Jewish people for four hundred years. Although this subjugation was destined for the Jewish people, the role of subjugation could have gone to any number of kings. Because he escorted Avraham and Sarah, Pharaoh received it.

In *Sefer Shoftim* we find that the tribes of Efrayim and Menasheh could not find the entrance to the city of Beis El when they went to conquer it (*Shoftim* 1:24). A person who lived in the city assisted them by showing them the entrance.

He was greatly rewarded for this act of virtue. Even though he did not even speak or move his feet, his life and his family were spared. In addition, Hashem helped him build the city Luz, which had a thriving economy of preparing the *techeiles* dye for tzitzis. The city was always protected from other nations, and no one ever died within the city limits.

Surely, the Gemara concludes, one who escorts others by actually walking along with them on foot will merit an even greater reward.

Rambam (*Hilchos Aveil* 14:2) teaches that the rewards for escorting a guest are greater than the rewards for all other forms of kindness. This was the great teaching that Avraham Avinu taught and lived by. He would feed passersby and escort them on their way. His inviting guests was considered greater than greeting the Divine Presence, yet his escorting them was even greater!

In a third incident, the citizens of Yericho failed to escort the prophet Elisha out of their city.

A group of forty-two youths began to ridicule the unescorted prophet, and they were punished with death (*Melachim* II 2:23–24). This could have been prevented if the townspeople had escorted Elisha. Thus, we learn that one who does not escort a traveler is considered as one who sheds blood.

Even in our daily lives, when we take a few steps with a guest we are building up his self-esteem and giving him encouragement. This brings honor to Hashem's name and gives the person the lift he needs to get through the day. One little act of kindness, done with our feet, can even save a person's life.

Chapter Nineteen

The Shoe Connection

The topic of appreciating all that shoes represent is a vast and profound one. We have attempted here to outline some aspects of this topic and some of its many ramifications.

A verse in *Shir HaShirim* (6:6) gives us another insight into our shoes. The verse mentions sheep, *recheilim*, and the question arises: Why would one of the great matriarchs be named *Rachel*, singular of *sheep*? We use this name for women extensively to this day. What is its significance?

Rashi on this verse explains that a sheep is an animal used entirely for mitzvos. Six parts of it are used for sacred purposes:

- The wool for *techeiles* in tzitzis and for the garments of the *kohein gadol*
- The animal's flesh for sacrifices that were brought on the *mizbei'ach*

- The horns for shofars which we blow on Rosh HaShanah and in the Beis HaMikdash

- The leg bones for flutes which the Levi'im used to play in the Beis HaMikdash

- The intestines for harp strings, also used for the Levi'im's orchestra music

- The hides for the drums and tambourines also used by the Levi'im

What a concept! We see a picture of total devotion to Hashem. Not only is the bulk of the animal used for a *korban*, but also every part of it is dedicated to serving Hashem — from the outside to the inside, from top to bottom!

Similarly, when we make shoes out of leather, we demonstrate how we use every part of an animal to serve Hashem. We can learn from this how all of our actions should be for the sake of Heaven, as the Mishnah teaches (*Avos* 2:17). The Gemara (*Berachos* 64a) says on the verse "In all your ways know Him" (*Mishlei* 3:6) that the whole Torah is dependent on this principle — doing everything for the sake of Hashem.

Where do we find a parallel to this concept in Hashem's behavior toward us?

Rav Yitzchak Hutner (*Pachad Yitzchak*, Purim

Many years later, when he was celebrating the completion of one of his great *sefarim*, he told his story. He commented: "Had I settled for being a shoemaker, after 120 years the Heavenly Tribunal would have taken me to task for not having written these great *sefarim* that I had the potential to write."

Part two is a story involving Rav Yitzchak Hutner, *zt"l*. A person proudly showed a *sefer* he had written to Rav Hutner, who studied the *sefer* and was dismayed at how poorly it was written and constructed. Rav Hutner subsequently told a student, "When a person writes a *sefer* of inferior quality because he is not fit for such an accomplishment, he may be taken to task after 120 years with the question, 'Where are all the fine quality shoes you could have produced?' "

Each person has his mission in life. We have to develop our potential and justify our existence. It may be that producing shoes according to Torah guidelines is one person's greatness and is as important as another person's *sefer*.

There is no difference between one who does more and one who does less, as long as his intentions are for the sake of Heaven.

(Menachos 110a)

Putting on Shoe:

The Gemara (*Shabbos* 61a) teaches us how to put on shoes: First put on the right shoe without tying the lace, then put on the left shoe and tie it, and finally tie the right one. (Note: There is a dispute whether this halachah applies to women.)

The *Shulchan Aruch* records these instructions in *Orach Chaim* 2:4. *Mishnah Berurah* explains that the Torah is teaching us to recognize the importance of our right side in all matters, with the exception of tying, where we honor the left side first because one's tefillin is worn on his left arm. (A left-handed person who wears his tefillin on his right arm should tie his right shoe first.)

When removing one's shoes, one should remove his left one first to honor the right one.

It is interesting to note that the basic concept of wearing shoes daily is taught in the *Shulchan Aruch* (*Orach Chaim* 2:6): "Do not walk around barefoot." The *Mishnah Berurah* explains that this is based on the Talmudic teaching that one should sell all of his possessions if necessary in order to buy shoes. We should always wear shoes, unless one is going barefoot to repent his sins, as we do on Yom Kippur.

In *Hilchos Shabbos* (301:62), the *Mishnah Berurah* explains that the reason for wearing shoes daily is because it is modest to cover all parts of one's body, including the feet. The *Shulchan Aruch* (301:16) teaches that it is even more important not to go barefoot on Shabbos. The *Mishnah Berurah* gives two reasons for this:

- To help one remember that it is Shabbos. This would be a source for one to have a special pair of shoes for Shabbos. (In paragraph 262, the *Mishnah Berurah* teaches that it is ideal for a person to change all of his clothing in honor of Shabbos.)

- To enhance the pleasure of Shabbos.

The Talmud (*Chullin* 9b) teaches that a person does not even stub his toe unless it was decreed in Heaven. Perhaps one of the reasons for this Heavenly proclamation is to chastise the person for failing to wear shoes to protect his feet.

Chapter Twenty-two

Step by Step

When we study the halachah of putting on shoes in depth, we find that it is not so simple. Although Rabbi Yochanan states in *Maseches Shabbos* (61a) that just as one puts tefillin on his left arm, he should put on his left shoe first, there is another source, a *beraisa*, that teaches that one should put on his right shoe first. The Gemara (ibid.) deals with reconciling these two conflicting sources. According to Rabbi Yosef, either way is acceptable, whereas Rabbi Nachman bar Yitzchak suggests to put the right shoe on first but tie the left one first.

Tosafos points out that we find that the right side of the body is significant in certain laws of the Torah. For example, when the Mishkan service was inaugurated, the Torah records, "Moshe took of [the ram's] blood to apply to the edge of Aaron's right ear, the thumb of his right hand, and the large toe of his right foot" (*Vayikra* 8:23).

Putting on the right shoe first is a reminder that we should always strive to be on the "right" side in life. Shlomo HaMelech teaches, "A wise person's heart is on the right" (*Koheles* 10:2).

On the other hand, the left side reminds us of how much we cherish the mitzvah of tefillin, which contain the paragraphs of Shema and teach the basic principles of belief in Hashem's Oneness, His greatness, and His power. Why do we wear tefillin on our left arm? Rav Reuven Feinstein, *shlita*, teaches that perhaps it is to teach us that we should always fortify ourselves and strive to strengthen our weaknesses.

The conclusion of the *Shulchan Aruch* is as follows: One should put on his right shoe first without tying the lace, and then put on the left one. He should then tie the left one and then the right one.

If one's shoes do not have laces, the right one should be put on first.

A left-handed person should tie his right shoe first.

When removing shoes, one should remove his left shoe first.

It is permitted to put on two layers of footwear (such as shoes and boots) at the same time (*Aruch HaShulchan* 6).

Chapter Twenty-three

Touching Shoes

"One who handles his shoes as he removes them has to wash his hands" (*Shulchan Aruch* 4:18).

The *Mishnah Berurah* explains that the purpose of this washing is cleanliness, so there is no rush to wash immediately. After handling new shoes, one does not need to wash at all (*Kaf HaChaim* 61).

The Chazon Ish is quoted as saying that one does not have to wash his hands at all if he only touched shoelaces (Rabbi Yosef Y. Lerner, *Shemiras HaGuf VeHaNefesh*, p. 173).

Kohanim remove their shoes before blessing the congregation in shul. When they put them back on, the *Orach Chaim* cautions, they should not touch them. If they do, they should wash their hands before continuing their prayers (*Orach Chaim* 128:17).

The *Mishnah Berurah* explains that this is necessary no matter what type of shoe a *kohein* is wearing because all shoes are considered to have some dust or dirt on them. Even if the shoes are clean and shiny, one needs to wash his hands after touching them because they have a *ruach ra*, a form of defilement (*Shulchan Aruch HaRav* 128:27).

Chapter Twenty-four

A Closer Look at Handling Shoes

We learned above that the *Shulchan Aruch* requires one who removes his shoes to wash his hands (*Orach Chaim* 4:18). Does this mean that one must wash his entire hand or can he wash only the part that touched the shoe?

The *Mishnah Berurah* (#38) explains that when one gets some plain dirt on his fingers he only has to wash off the dirt. We can connect the *Mishnah Berurah*'s statement, quoted above, that washing hands after handling shoes is not an issue of removing evil spirits but of cleanliness. One would thus only have to wash the part of his hand which touched his shoe in order to clean it.

This fits with the *Mishnah Berurah*'s statement in paragraph 614:14 that someone who has to wear shoes on Yom Kippur should not touch them with bare hands. If he does so, he must wash the part of his hand which touched the shoes.

Why does the *Shulchan Aruch* say, "One who *removes* his shoes needs to wash his hands," when it could have simply said, "One who touches his shoes"?

The *sefer Mor U'Ketzia* explains that this phraseology was used to exclude new shoes that were not worn yet. Only after shoes are worn the first time do they become enveloped with a *ruach ra*.

This is explained more in *Responsa of Yabia Omer* (5:1), based on the verse, "Accursed is the soil" (*Bereishis* 3:17). Because of this curse, there are evil spirits upon the earth which can cling to shoes and to feet. This is the reason why Sephardim avoid going barefoot, even on Tishah B'Av. They are careful to always wear shoes or some other foot covering in order to avoid contact with the earth's *ruach ra*.

According to this view, washing is required not because of cleanliness, but to avoid being affected by the *ruach ra*. Most Ashkenazim do not follow this view.

Chapter Twenty-five

Shoes on Shabbos

There are numerous halachos that apply to shoes on Shabbos. One must be careful to avoid transgressing prohibitions such as knotting, fixing professionally, and *muktzeh*. Many applications of these important halachos are outlined below.

Shoelaces

One may tie his shoelaces with a single knot followed by a bow, if he will be opening it up within twenty-four hours (*Shulchan Aruch* 317:5). A tight double knot, like those often made for children's shoes, should not be tied or untied on Shabbos (ibid. 317:1). However, untying is permitted if the knot is a cause of *tzaar* (pain).

One may reinsert shoelaces that were removed from a shoe, without making any knots, if it is not a difficult process. However, one may not in-

HaShulchan 327:4). Others argue that it is better not to use a cloth and to only dust the shoe off by hand or by stamping the foot.

One may not smear oil on leather shoes because it softens the leather (ibid.). Nor may one bend the leather by hand in order to soften it.

If one has some mud on his shoe, he may rub it off against a wall, but according to the Rambam it should not be rubbed on the ground. However, Rosh permits rubbing a shoe on the ground (*Shulchan Aruch* 302:6).

The *Mishnah Berurah* explains that all agree that it is prohibited to use any form of metal scraper, knife handle, or floor stand. One may use the wall, a beam, or the edge of a step. If one rubs gently or the mud is moist, it may be less of a problem, but one should look into the halachos carefully.

One may pour water on a shoe in order to clean it off, but he may not rub it clean (ibid. 302:9). If a shoe has fabric on it, water should not be poured on it.

Chapter Twenty-seven

Shoes on Yom Kippur

One may not wear leather shoes on Yom Kippur. This prohibition applies even if only part of the shoe is leather, whether the leather is on the bottom or on the top, and there is no difference whether the leather is soft or hard. It also applies to both men and women.

One may wear nonleather footwear, such as of rubber or cloth. Some say one should not wear sneakers which are as comfortable as leather shoes (*Mishnah Berurah* 5), unless one is not well or elderly.

One may stand on a leather mat, but some say it is better not to.

A woman within thirty days of giving birth may wear leather shoes if she needs them for health reasons. The same applies to others in need due to illness or other, similar reasons.

If one foot is injured, requiring a leather shoe,

nly that foot is exempt; the other foot is prohib-
ted from wearing leather (*Biur Halachah* and
Aruch HaShulchan).

Shoes are considered *muktzeh* on Yom Kippur, and one who wears them outside is considered carrying (*Minchas Chinuch*, *mitzvah* 313).

One may wear nonleather slippers on Yom
Kippur. However, he may not wear them in the
street if they can fall off and he may come to carry
them (*Orach Chaim* 301:16).

One should not dress his children with
leather footwear on Yom Kippur.

The *Shulchan Aruch* says that children are
permitted to eat, drink, wash, and use ointments
on Yom Kippur, but they should not wear leather
shoes (*Orach Chaim* 616:1). The *Mishnah Berurah*
(611:3) says that it is proper to be stringent and
consider the prohibition against wearing leather
shoes on Yom Kippur a Torah law. Thus, we are
careful even with children.

Shoes on Chol HaMo'ec

Although professional shoe repair is prohib
ited on Chol HaMo'ed, one may make cer
tain light, nonprofessional repairs to his
shoes on Chol HaMo'ed for the sake of wearing
them on the mo'ed (*Orach Chaim* 541).

If one is suffering from the rain or from thorns
because of his torn shoes, and he has no other
shoes, he may even have them repaired by a shoemaker. Similarly, if one's shoe might tear more
and become ruined beyond repair if he waits, he
may have it repaired on Chol HaMo'ed (*Mishnah
Berurah* 10).

Tosafos (on *Pesachim* 55b) explains that it is
better to buy new shoes on Chol HaMo'ed than to
repair a torn pair (*Shaar HaTzion* 16).

Some say it is prohibited to polish shoes on
Chol HaMo'ed because of the prohibition against
doing laundry or because of the prohibition

against repairing a shoe. The Chazon Ish held one should avoid it (*Mo'adim U'Zemanim* 7:154). Some allow having it done by a non-Jew. Rav Moshe Feinstein, *zt"l*, says it is better to avoid polishing shoes unless it is a desperate situation (*sha'as hadechak*). All agree that one may use a brush or a rag without any polish.

One may not have worn heels or soles replaced by a shoemaker (Jew or non-Jew) on Chol HaMo'ed even if he needs the shoes for *yom tov* (*Orach Chaim* 541:4).

If one's only pair of shoes will be completely ruined if they are not fixed immediately, he may have them repaired on Chol HaMo'ed, even by a professional (*Mishnah Berurah* 541:10). If possible, it is better to purchase a new pair of shoes on Chol HaMo'ed than to repair the old pair (*Shaar HaTziyun*).

If the shoes were repaired before *yom tov*, one may pick them up on Chol HaMo'ed if he will wear them for *yom tov* (*Orach Chaim* 534:3). He should not drop shoes off at a repair shop on Chol HaMo'ed to have them repaired after *yom tov*.

Chapter Twenty-nine

Miscellaneous Shoe Halachos

One should not sleep with shoes on because it can cause him to taste the flavor of death (*Yoma* 78b).

One should not even allow children to sleep with their shoes on.

Kaf HaChaim (*Yoreh Dei'ah* 116:211) says that this applies also to sandals or slippers.

Some say that one should not wear shoes that were inherited from a person who died (*Sefer Chassidim* 454). One explanation for this is that it may cause him to dream about the deceased coming to claim his shoes. The Gemara (*Berachos* 57b) teaches that if a person dreams that a deceased person came to take something it is a good sign, but not if he came to take shoes. This can be explained with the three approaches we have mentioned above regarding the significance of shoes in general. (See chapters 1, 10, and 14. Shoes demonstrate our ability to go out and accomplish in the world; they signify our superior status; and they symbolize the body which protects the soul. Thus, taking them away has a negative connotation.)

The *Iggros Moshe* (on *Yoreh Dei'ah* 3:133) explains that this only applies to a case where the cause of death is unknown and it may have been a contagious disease which can be transmitted by the deceased's shoes to others.

One should not wear tight shoes, as they may cause illness (*Kaf HaChaim, Yoreh Dei'ah* 16:171).

Some say that one should not polish his shoes on the day he sets out on a trip. It should be done the day before (*Kaf HaChaim, Orach Chaim* 110:22 and *Yoreh Dei'ah* 116:163). One of the explanations for this custom is that a person should always prepare himself in advance, as the Mishnah teaches, "Repent the day before you depart from this world" (*Avos* 2:9). (See *Shemiras HaGuf VeHaNefesh*, p. 295.)

One should not pray with his head or feet uncovered if he would not present himself in front of dignified people in such a manner (*Orach Chaim* 91:5).

If it is raining or snowing and one comes to shul with rubbers or boots, he should consider whether it is proper to leave them on for prayers. If you were meeting with an important dignitary, would you leave your boots on during the meeting?

Part Two

Ten Blessings

Gift of a Mind

Since the blessing for shoes is the tenth in the list of blessings we recite every morning, we can view the previous nine blessings as a buildup to the all-encompassing blessing for shoes — "Hashem…has provided me with all my needs." Each step of the way helps us to appreciate another of Hashem's gifts to us.

The first *berachah* is a thanks for "giving my heart the ability to distinguish between day and night," which is the gift of the mind. Hashem provides us our ability to think and analyze, our curiosity and desire to learn about the world around us. We are able to keep growing because we can think, observe what is around us, and learn Torah.

Learning is a process of absorbing information and then applying it and living with it. The fundamental key to all education is the desire and thirst for learning. Discerning between night and day can only be accomplished if we learn. We seek to illuminate our minds and hearts with Torah — Hashem's instructions and guidance in all areas of life.

Before we thank Hashem for our shoes, we acknowledge that we are grateful for the gift of our mind and our understanding. The first *berachah* is for the mind because the mind is the starting point for everything that we want to accomplish in life. Just like seeds need to be watered, fertilized, and cultivated to grow into reality, we need to dream about our goals and develop them in our minds so that we can accomplish them, with Hashem's help.

Gift of Identity

W hen we begin our thinking process, we need to dwell on who we are. Thus, it is appropriate that the second blessing is a thanks for "having not made me a non-Jew." Our lives become enriched with meaning when we realize how fortunate we are to be part of the Chosen People.

Often we wake up in the morning yearning to accomplish so much — but we must first dwell on that which we already have. Let us remember how beloved we are as people created in Hashem's image, and how much more beloved we are since we are considered Hashem's children (*Avos* 3:18). We will always be in good spirits if we learn to appreciate the priceless gift of our Jewish identity.

The overwhelming feeling of gratitude for our unique status should be as much a part of us as breathing and thinking. As Jews, we are granted

the opportunity to perform 613 mitzvos, a privi
lege not given to the rest of humanity, which ha
only seven mitzvos. Each mitzvah brings us close
to our Creator. We must realize that the most im
portant aspect of life, above even health, family
and wealth, is our spirituality, our connection to
Hashem.

Gift of Freedom

Once we proudly identify ourselves as Jews and thank Hashem for this privileged status, we proceed to the third blessing: "who has not made me a servant."

We are Hashem's servants, not servants to people (*Kiddushin* 22b). Every Jew must say this blessing and appreciate the freedom he enjoys every day.

What are we to use this freedom for? "The only free person is one who studies Torah" (*Avos* 6:2).

Who are you subservient to in your daily life? Do you properly utilize your freedom? There is a saying, "In America there is a Statue of Liberty, but they also need a Statue of Responsibility." The Torah teaches us that liberty must be linked with responsibility. We have a responsibility to Hashem and His Torah which we cannot shirk.

When we wake up in the morning, before we

consider the benefits of our shoes, we need to decide who we are as people. We are not slaves. This awareness can give us direction in life, as well as elevated priorities and goals. With the right Torah attitude, we will gain tremendously over time, both in the physical and spiritual realms.

Gift of More Mitzvah Opportunities

Our gift of freedom is naturally followed by another gift — the gift of more mitzvah opportunities, for a man, or the gift of a unique connection to Hashem, for a woman.

Each of us was sent to this world by Hashem to accomplish great things in his own individual way. We have been charged with a mission, and we can make a difference in many people's lives, if we begin by appreciating who Hashem created us to be.

When you are aware of and focused on developing your full potential, you will feel as comfortable as you are wearing your own shoes. Ask yourself, *Am I wearing the right shoes for who I am?* If the answer is yes, be grateful to Hashem for this great gift, the fourth on our list of incredible gifts.

You were born in a particular circumstance to special parents and a special environment. You were given a unique personality and a bevy of talents, abilities, and challenges. Your dreams and goals challenge you and motivate you so that you can dedicate your energy and resources for positive purposes.

The future is open to us.

Gift of Clothing

Why does the blessing for clothing follow the one for eyesight? One obvious answer is that when clothing was first introduced to mankind by Adam and Chavah, it came as a result of the "opening of the eyes of both of them" (*Bereishis* 3:7).

Hashem clothed the first man and his wife (ibid. 3:21) to teach us that we must cover our bodies. "The exterior stimulates the interior" (*Mesilas Yesharim*, ch. 7). By wearing dignified clothing we remind ourselves of our dignity as human beings, created in the image of Hashem. Before the sin, Adam recognized his inner dignity without clothing, but after it he needed clothing to protect him from temptation and to remind him that man is unique in the Universe, with an eternal soul that Hashem blew into him. We cover our body to conceal the physical part of us, which is more animal-like.

This *berachah* reminds us of Hashem's kindness in giving us clothing and also of our unique qualities and corresponding responsibilities (Rav Avigdor Miller, *The Beginning*, p. 104). One reason that this blessing for clothing follows the one for eyesight is that although eyesight is a wonderful blessing, it is vital to know what to avoid.

When you dress in a dignified manner, you recognize who you are created to be and what you can become. As a human being, you can achieve greatness!

Gift of Mobility

In our next blessing, we thank Hashem for "releasing the bound." This refers to our ability to move around, to move our muscles and limbs. None of us is tied down; we can determine exactly where we want to go and how to get there.

It is comfortable to lie in bed and hold onto a pillow or security blanket. But to succeed in life we must leave our comfort zone and take some risks. "According to the difficulties, so are the rewards" (*Avos* 5:23). The more we battle against laziness, the more we will achieve in Torah and mitzvos.

As we walk on the path of service to Hashem, we must recognize that it is He who gives us the ability to move about from place to place. It is easy to take this ability for granted as we involve ourselves in a myriad of daily activities. Stop each morning and remember that you would have no use for shoes if you were tied down!

Hashem releases us from all types of chains to enable us to achieve. When we confront barriers and limitations, we need to remember that all relief comes from Hashem. He releases those who are bound and He will provide all of your needs if you are working with Him.

Gift of Upright Posture

After thanking Hashem for our mobility, we go on to bless Him for "straightening the bent," giving us the ability to stand erect. Why does Hashem enable us to stand erect? Although we could have lived on all fours as animals with intelligence, Hashem wants us to live with dignity. In order to emulate Hashem and live lives of elevation, perfection, and holiness, we need to stand straight and tall.

When we stand upright, we have the enthusiasm and energy we need for studying and practicing Torah, serving Hashem through prayer, and helping others. We can take control of our lives when our heads are on top — controlling our desires.

When you stand erect, you can see farther down the road of life. You can look ahead and visualize yourself living at a higher level. You have the power to turn your desires into specific goals and plans. For all this, we need to thank Hashem.

Who is wise? He who foresees that which will develop.

(*Tamid* 32a)

Both the blessing for mobility and this one, for upright posture, remind us that it is time to remove the shackles that are tying us down. Look ahead to each new day with confidence in Hashem's help and awareness of your inner dignity and uniqueness.

Gift of the Ground

There is another essential component, for which we thank Hashem in blessing number nine: "He who spreads the earth upon the water."

Why do we thank Hashem for firmly establishing the earth immediately after we thank for our upright posture? It is not enough to merely know what you desire, set your eyes on your goals, and stand up straight with the confidence that you can achieve those goals. The next step is to set your feet on the ground.

Your intentions may be wonderful, but in order to carry out your plans, you need to be grounded.

On the path one desires to go, he will be led.
(*Makkos* 10b)

Hashem is ready and waiting to guide us, to

lead us by the hand, so to speak — but first we need to choose the path on which we will go. Put your feet on the floor, put on your shoes, and decide your direction.

The obstacles and challenges in life may be compared to ditches, water holes, or quicksand. But Hashem is the One who spreads the earth over the water. He builds the bridges to get us over the holes to reach the goals we aspire to.

Gift of Shoes

Hashem has provided me with all of my needs.

This is the only *berachah* that emphasizes "me." Hashem has provided me with all of my needs, a program tailor-made just for me.

Pirkei Avos teaches, "If I am not for myself, who will be for me?" (*Avos* 1:14). Each of us is a unique, one-of-a-kind individual. We need to focus on our own talents and abilities and keep saying, *Why not me? And why not now?*

When we thank Hashem for all the gifts He has blessed us with, we are energized and motivated to make something special out of the day ahead of us. It is important to slow down at the word *li*, for me. What is my dream for my life? What excites and intrigues me?

Each of us walks in his own shoes. If our shoes don't fit properly, they will hurt our feet!

If we fail at something and then blame others, we are making a mistake. It helps to look down at your shoes and think back to all of the decisions you made that led you to this point. Most of the time, you get what you choose. And if what you've gotten does not suit you, you still have the ability to choose how to respond to it.

Hashem is the One who provides you with shoes that fit. But He doesn't leave you to walk alone after that. The next blessing is "He prepares man's footsteps."

Let us return to the question of why shoes are considered the number-one, all-encompassing gift that Hashem provides us with, to the extent that they are called "all of my needs." Perhaps it is because they enable us to begin traveling the road to greatness, with the knowledge that with Hashem's help we will succeed.

Why not me? And why not now?

Epilogue

We will conclude with some fundamental lessons that summarize many of the ideas presented in this book and also provide a few new insights.

- Shoes help us become individuals capable of standing on our own two feet, with Hashem's help. We should not belittle or pity ourselves. "If I am not for myself, who will be for me?" (*Avos* 1:14).

- As you put on your shoes, brace yourself and map out your goals for the day. You can face your challenges in life. It is easy if you focus on one footstep at a time. Eventually, miles of success are achieved.

- Our two feet match each other. This reminds us that we can influence others by treating them in the same manner that we would like

them to treat us. When we smile at others
they respond in kind. When we make efforts
to find a quality to praise in others, they recip
rocate in kind.

- There are two sides to life. We have good days
and we have days where the trials seem overwhelming. Let us remember that tests serve to
guide us toward improvement. Hashem wants
us to be balanced on two feet, striding forward
even in the face of adversity.

- "According to the difficulties, so are the rewards" (*Avos* 5:23). When things are difficult,
we should not make excuses. Instead, let us
learn to improve, to do more and give more.
Put on your shoes to go do that which
Hashem desires of you.

- Your two feet cannot go in two directions at
the same time. What a valuable life lesson!
Don't waste time hesitating between your
goals. You will never accomplish anything
great that way. When you concentrate on one
goal at a time, with both feet, you advance.

- Shoes are commonplace. We have been at-
tempting in this book to study the great lessons inherent even in simple commodities, an

endeavor which can be applied to any area of life. Think of a small, everyday object or activity. What can you learn from it?

Shoes bring to mind one of the great truths of the Talmud: "Every individual is obligated to say, 'Hashem created the entire universe because of me'" (*Sanhedrin* 37a). Shoes represent utilizing all materials for the benefit of people. Hashem is promoting and elevating me — do I accept the message?

It is important to keep in mind that the blessing, "who has provided me with all my needs," is far more profound than what we can explain in this small book. Our prayers and blessings are the keys that unlock Hashem's treasure-houses for us. Let us always continue to pray to Hashem, our Creator, for all our needs, and strive to continue gaining deeper understanding of the profound words of our prayers.